Bertha

Julie Mitchell
Mal Chambers

Rigby

www.Rigby.com
1-800-531-5015

Rigby Focus Forward

This Edition © 2009 Rigby, a Harcourt Education Imprint

Published in 2007 by Nelson Australia Pty Ltd ACN: 058 280 149
A Cengage Learning company

1 2 3 4 5 6 7 8 374 14 13 12 11 10 09 08 07
Printed and bound in China

Bertha
ISBN-13   978-1-4190-3703-0
ISBN-10   1-4190-3703-X

Bertha

Julie Mitchell
Mal Chambers

Contents

Chapter 1

A New Car!

"It's time we got a new car," said Dad.
"Bertha's getting old,
and she needs a lot of work."

"Can we get a pink car?"
asked Maddy, my sister.
"A pink car would go
with my new jacket."

"How about purple, Dad?" I asked.
"A purple car would be cool."

"I'd like a black one, Jake," Dad said.
"Black cars always look good."

"Black's too dark," Mom said.
"People won't see us coming.
Let's get a yellow car."

6

"We'll go and look at new cars,"
Dad said.
"We can pick one that we all like."

Chapter 2

Keeping Bertha

Mom, Dad, and Maddy
liked the first car we tried out.
But I didn't.

"My legs are stuck," I said.
"This car doesn't have
as much room as Bertha."

We took another car out for a test drive.
"It runs well," Mom said,
"but the seats are a bit hard.
Bertha's seats are nice and soft."

Everyone liked the next car,
until Dad tried out its horn.
"Oh," Maddy said, "that sounds terrible.
I like Bertha's horn more."

Dad bumped his head
in the last car.
After that, we went home.

Dad didn't say anymore
about a new car.
We kept Bertha
and went everywhere in her.

Chapter 3

The Right Car

As time passed,
Bertha's paint began to peel,
and her sides got rusty.

Bertha looked so bad
that Maddy and I
didn't want anyone
to see us in her.
When her tailpipe fell off
outside our school,
we couldn't stand it anymore.

"Dad," said Maddy,
"we *have* to get a new car!"

"And *soon*," I said.
"Bertha's falling to pieces!"

"You're right," Dad said.
"We'll get one over the holidays."

We went away for the first week
of the holidays.
When we came back,
we took a taxi home from the airport.

"Can we look for a new car, Dad?"
I asked.

"We don't need to,"
he said, smiling.
"There's a new car waiting for us
at home."

What a shock!
But as soon as we got over the shock,
we all started talking at one time.

"Is it yellow with soft seats?"
Mom asked.

"Is it pink?" asked Maddy.
"What does the horn sound like?"

"Is it purple with lots of room?"
I asked.
"Or is it black?"

Dad smiled again.
"Wait and see," he said.
"You're all going to love this car."

And we did!